MANIFESTATION JOURNAL

VISION *Board*

MANIFESTATION *Board*

FINANCE

CAREER

TRAVEL

MANIFESTATION *Board*

FAMILY

LOVE

HOME

HEALTH

LOVE *Manifestations*

WHAT I WANT TO MANIFEST

WHY I WANT TO MANIFEST

HOW WILL I MANIFEST IT

SMALL STEPS TO BEGIN

FAMILY *Manifestations*

WHAT I WANT TO MANIFEST

WHY I WANT TO MANIFEST

HOW WILL I MANIFEST IT

SMALL STEPS TO BEGIN

HOME *Manifestations*

WHAT I WANT TO MANIFEST

WHY I WANT TO MANIFEST

HOW WILL I MANIFEST IT

SMALL STEPS TO BEGIN

CAREER *Manifestations*

WHAT I WANT TO MANIFEST

WHY I WANT TO MANIFEST

HOW WILL I MANIFEST IT

SMALL STEPS TO BEGIN

HEALTH *Manifestations*

WHAT I WANT TO MANIFEST

WHY I WANT TO MANIFEST

HOW WILL I MANIFEST IT

SMALL STEPS TO BEGIN

FINANCE *Manifestations*

WHAT I WANT TO MANIFEST

WHY I WANT TO MANIFEST

HOW WILL I MANIFEST IT

SMALL STEPS TO BEGIN

TRAVEL *Manifestations*

WHAT I WANT TO MANIFEST

WHY I WANT TO MANIFEST

HOW WILL I MANIFEST IT

SMALL STEPS TO BEGIN

MORE *Manifestations*

WHAT I WANT TO MANIFEST

WHY I WANT TO MANIFEST

HOW WILL I MANIFEST IT

SMALL STEPS TO BEGIN

AFFIRMATION *Cards*

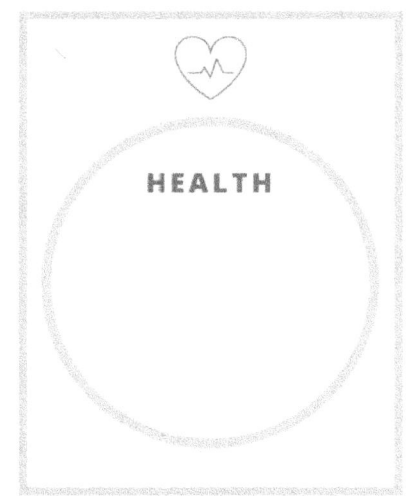
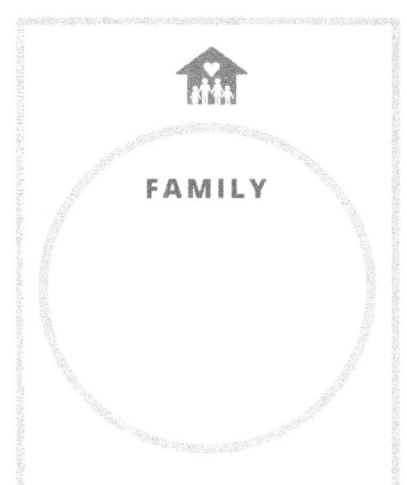

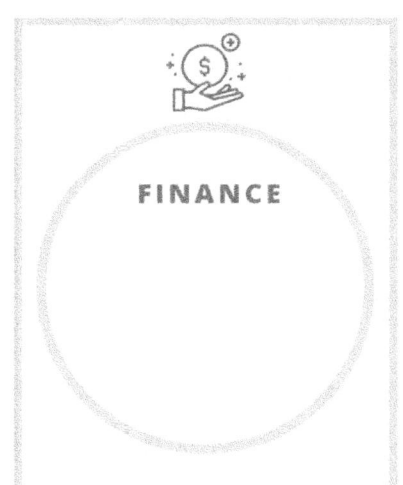

LIFE *Updates*

FAMILY UPDATES & CHANGES

LOVE UPDATES & CHANGES

HOME UPDATES & CHANGES

LIFE *Updates*

FINANCE UPDATES & CHANGES

CAREER UPDATES & CHANGES

TRAVEL UPDATES & CHANGES

LIFE *Updates*

HEALTH UPDATES & CHANGES

Notes

Notes

Notes

Notes

Notes

VISION Board

MANIFESTATION Board

FINANCE

CAREER

TRAVEL

MANIFESTATION *Board*

FAMILY

LOVE

HOME

HEALTH

LOVE *Manifestations*

WHAT I WANT TO MANIFEST

WHY I WANT TO MANIFEST

HOW WILL I MANIFEST IT

SMALL STEPS TO BEGIN

FAMILY *Manifestations*

WHAT I WANT TO MANIFEST

WHY I WANT TO MANIFEST

HOW WILL I MANIFEST IT

SMALL STEPS TO BEGIN

HOME *Manifestations*

WHAT I WANT TO MANIFEST

WHY I WANT TO MANIFEST

HOW WILL I MANIFEST IT

SMALL STEPS TO BEGIN

CAREER *Manifestations*

WHAT I WANT TO MANIFEST

WHY I WANT TO MANIFEST

HOW WILL I MANIFEST IT

SMALL STEPS TO BEGIN

HEALTH *Manifestations*

WHAT I WANT TO MANIFEST

WHY I WANT TO MANIFEST

HOW WILL I MANIFEST IT

SMALL STEPS TO BEGIN

FINANCE *Manifestations*

WHAT I WANT TO MANIFEST

WHY I WANT TO MANIFEST

HOW WILL I MANIFEST IT

SMALL STEPS TO BEGIN

TRAVEL *Manifestations*

WHAT I WANT TO MANIFEST

WHY I WANT TO MANIFEST

HOW WILL I MANIFEST IT

SMALL STEPS TO BEGIN

MORE *Manifestations*

WHAT I WANT TO MANIFEST

WHY I WANT TO MANIFEST

HOW WILL I MANIFEST IT

SMALL STEPS TO BEGIN

AFFIRMATION *Cards*

HEALTH	FAMILY	TRAVEL
CAREER	FINANCE	LOVE
HOME		

LIFE *Updates*

FAMILY UPDATES & CHANGES

LOVE UPDATES & CHANGES

HOME UPDATES & CHANGES

LIFE *Updates*

FINANCE UPDATES & CHANGES

CAREER UPDATES & CHANGES

TRAVEL UPDATES & CHANGES

LIFE *Updates*

HEALTH UPDATES & CHANGES

Notes

Notes

Notes

Notes

Notes

VISION *Board*

MANIFESTATION *Board*

FINANCE

CAREER

TRAVEL

MANIFESTATION *Board*

FAMILY

LOVE

HOME

HEALTH

LOVE *Manifestations*

WHAT I WANT TO MANIFEST

WHY I WANT TO MANIFEST

HOW WILL I MANIFEST IT

SMALL STEPS TO BEGIN

FAMILY *Manifestations*

WHAT I WANT TO MANIFEST

WHY I WANT TO MANIFEST

HOW WILL I MANIFEST IT

SMALL STEPS TO BEGIN

HOME *Manifestations*

WHAT I WANT TO MANIFEST

WHY I WANT TO MANIFEST

HOW WILL I MANIFEST IT

SMALL STEPS TO BEGIN

CAREER *Manifestations*

WHAT I WANT TO MANIFEST

WHY I WANT TO MANIFEST

HOW WILL I MANIFEST IT

SMALL STEPS TO BEGIN

HEALTH *Manifestations*

WHAT I WANT TO MANIFEST

WHY I WANT TO MANIFEST

HOW WILL I MANIFEST IT

SMALL STEPS TO BEGIN

FINANCE *Manifestations*

WHAT I WANT TO MANIFEST

WHY I WANT TO MANIFEST

HOW WILL I MANIFEST IT

SMALL STEPS TO BEGIN

TRAVEL *Manifestations*

WHAT I WANT TO MANIFEST

WHY I WANT TO MANIFEST

HOW WILL I MANIFEST IT

SMALL STEPS TO BEGIN

MORE *Manifestations*

WHAT I WANT TO MANIFEST

WHY I WANT TO MANIFEST

HOW WILL I MANIFEST IT

SMALL STEPS TO BEGIN

AFFIRMATION *Cards*

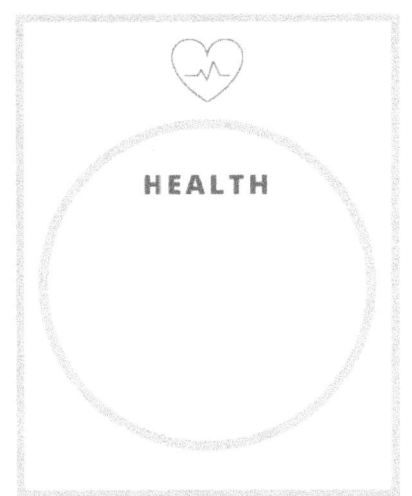
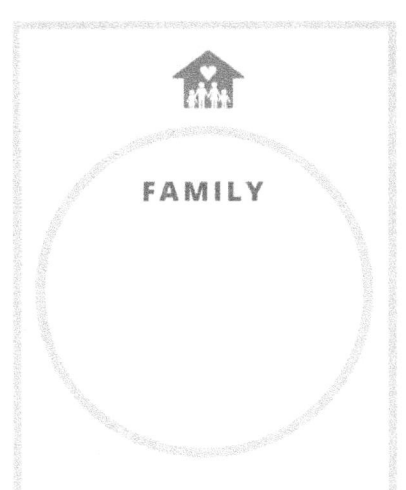

LIFE *Updates*

FAMILY UPDATES & CHANGES

LOVE UPDATES & CHANGES

HOME UPDATES & CHANGES

LIFE *Updates*

FINANCE UPDATES & CHANGES

CAREER UPDATES & CHANGES

TRAVEL UPDATES & CHANGES

LIFE *Updates*

HEALTH UPDATES & CHANGES

Notes

Notes

Notes

Notes

Notes

VISION *Board*

MANIFESTATION *Board*

FINANCE

CAREER

TRAVEL

MANIFESTATION *Board*

FAMILY

LOVE

HOME

HEALTH

LOVE *Manifestations*

WHAT I WANT TO MANIFEST

WHY I WANT TO MANIFEST

HOW WILL I MANIFEST IT

SMALL STEPS TO BEGIN

FAMILY *Manifestations*

WHAT I WANT TO MANIFEST

WHY I WANT TO MANIFEST

HOW WILL I MANIFEST IT

SMALL STEPS TO BEGIN

HOME *Manifestations*

WHAT I WANT TO MANIFEST

WHY I WANT TO MANIFEST

HOW WILL I MANIFEST IT

SMALL STEPS TO BEGIN

CAREER *Manifestations*

WHAT I WANT TO MANIFEST

WHY I WANT TO MANIFEST

HOW WILL I MANIFEST IT

SMALL STEPS TO BEGIN

HEALTH *Manifestations*

WHAT I WANT TO MANIFEST

WHY I WANT TO MANIFEST

HOW WILL I MANIFEST IT

SMALL STEPS TO BEGIN

FINANCE *Manifestations*

WHAT I WANT TO MANIFEST

WHY I WANT TO MANIFEST

HOW WILL I MANIFEST IT

SMALL STEPS TO BEGIN

TRAVEL *Manifestations*

WHAT I WANT TO MANIFEST

WHY I WANT TO MANIFEST

HOW WILL I MANIFEST IT

SMALL STEPS TO BEGIN

MORE *Manifestations*

WHAT I WANT TO MANIFEST

WHY I WANT TO MANIFEST

HOW WILL I MANIFEST IT

SMALL STEPS TO BEGIN

AFFIRMATION *Cards*

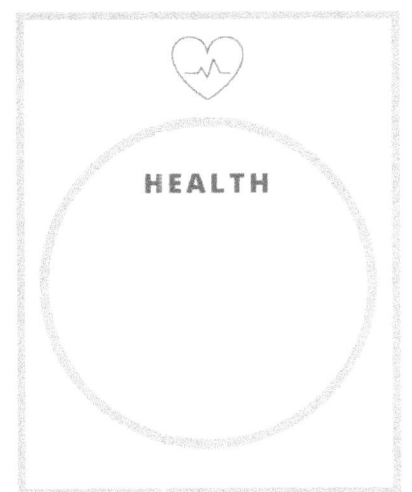
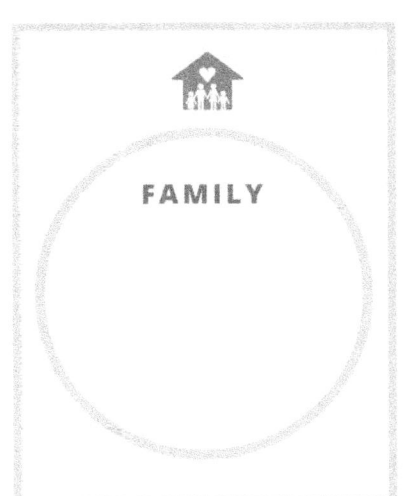

HEALTH **FAMILY** **TRAVEL**

CAREER **FINANCE** **LOVE**

HOME

LIFE *Updates*

FAMILY UPDATES & CHANGES

LOVE UPDATES & CHANGES

HOME UPDATES & CHANGES

LIFE Updates

FINANCE UPDATES & CHANGES

-
-
-
-
-

-
-
-
-
-

CAREER UPDATES & CHANGES

-
-
-
-
-

-
-
-
-
-

TRAVEL UPDATES & CHANGES

-
-
-
-
-

-
-
-
-
-

LIFE *Updates*

HEALTH UPDATES & CHANGES

Notes

Notes

Notes

Notes

Notes

VISION Board

MANIFESTATION *Board*

FINANCE

CAREER

TRAVEL

MANIFESTATION *Board*

FAMILY

LOVE

HOME

HEALTH

LOVE *Manifestations*

WHAT I WANT TO MANIFEST

WHY I WANT TO MANIFEST

HOW WILL I MANIFEST IT

SMALL STEPS TO BEGIN

FAMILY *Manifestations*

WHAT I WANT TO MANIFEST

WHY I WANT TO MANIFEST

HOW WILL I MANIFEST IT

SMALL STEPS TO BEGIN

HOME *Manifestations*

WHAT I WANT TO MANIFEST

WHY I WANT TO MANIFEST

HOW WILL I MANIFEST IT

SMALL STEPS TO BEGIN

CAREER *Manifestations*

WHAT I WANT TO MANIFEST

WHY I WANT TO MANIFEST

HOW WILL I MANIFEST IT

SMALL STEPS TO BEGIN

HEALTH *Manifestations*

WHAT I WANT TO MANIFEST

WHY I WANT TO MANIFEST

HOW WILL I MANIFEST IT

SMALL STEPS TO BEGIN

FINANCE *Manifestations*

WHAT I WANT TO MANIFEST

WHY I WANT TO MANIFEST

HOW WILL I MANIFEST IT

SMALL STEPS TO BEGIN

TRAVEL *Manifestations*

WHAT I WANT TO MANIFEST

WHY I WANT TO MANIFEST

HOW WILL I MANIFEST IT

SMALL STEPS TO BEGIN

MORE *Manifestations*

WHAT I WANT TO MANIFEST

WHY I WANT TO MANIFEST

HOW WILL I MANIFEST IT

SMALL STEPS TO BEGIN

AFFIRMATION *Cards*

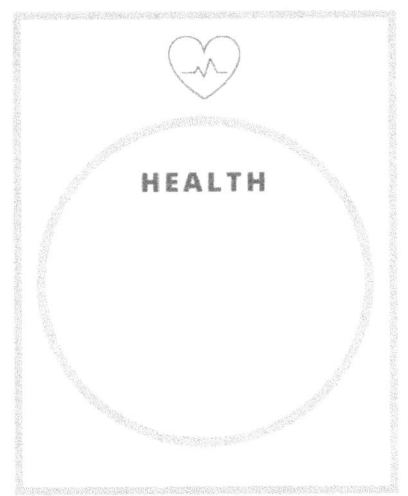
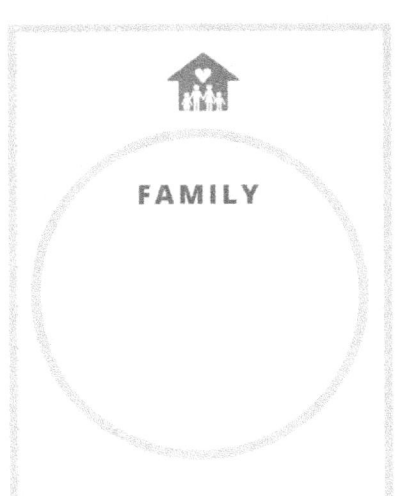

LIFE *Updates*

FAMILY UPDATES & CHANGES

LOVE UPDATES & CHANGES

HOME UPDATES & CHANGES

LIFE Updates

FINANCE UPDATES & CHANGES

-
-
-
-
-

-
-
-
-
-

CAREER UPDATES & CHANGES

-
-
-
-
-

-
-
-
-
-

TRAVEL UPDATES & CHANGES

-
-
-
-
-

-
-
-
-
-

LIFE *Updates*

HEALTH UPDATES & CHANGES

Notes

Notes

Notes

Notes